Distracted Globe

A comedy

N. J. Warburton

Samuel French—London
New York-Toronto-Hollywood

Please see page iv for further copyright information

DISTRACTED GLOBE

First performed at Stapleford, Cambridge, on 26th
February 1993, with the following cast:

Gerry	George Elsbury
Eric	Edward Sharrock
Patsy	Lynn Pepperell
Ophelia	Nicola Higgins
Alice	Val Furness
Kate	Margaret McCarthy

Directed by Jenni Sinclair

CHARACTERS

Gerry, stage manager
Eric, the ghost of Hamlet's father
Patsy, stage crew
Ophelia, Hamlet's friend
Alice, stage crew
Kate, producer

At the director's discretion, there may be other party-goers: non-speaking cast or crew who come on with Alice to have a few drinks and swell the ranks

PRODUCTION NOTE

Distracted Globe follows the fortunes of The Drama Group members from *Don't Blame It On The Boots* and *Easy Stages*. The Group has just presented *Hamlet*, with mixed success. Now is the chance for cast and crew to relax and enjoy the after-play party. The party takes place on the set of *Hamlet*, which was used in the above plays.

"Remember thee?
Ay, thou poor ghost, whiles memory holds a seat
In this distracted globe."

(*Hamlet,* Act I, Scene 5)

Hamlet is making a clever reference that works on a number of levels in this line. "Globe" might be taken to refer to:

    (i) the world spinning in space

    (ii) Hamlet's own head

    (iii) the theatre, *the* Globe, in which so many of Shakespeare's plays were performed

    (iv) a theatrical prop: a daring reference to the globe Mrs Tremlett was to lend a drama group four hundred years after the opening of the play

OTHER PLAYS BY N.J WARBURTON

Don't Blame It On The Boots
Easy Stages
Ghost Writer
The Loophole
Receive This Light
Sour Grapes and Ashes
Zartan

DISTRACTED GLOBE

Music is heard. It is "Morning" from Peer Gynt—or similar

The CURTAIN *swishes half open, stops, then swishes shut*

Pause

The CURTAIN *jerks open a yard or two and stops*

Gerry enters, walking briskly into the gap with a clipboard, muttering to himself and ticking off things anxiously on his list. He looks up and notices the CURTAIN. *He is annoyed and is about to say so, when the* CURTAIN *jerks again as if to close. Gerry flings his clipboard aside and leaps down stage to avoid the* CURTAIN

Eric guffaws at him from the auditorium

Gerry (*turning and shading his eyes*) Who's there?
Eric (*booming*) Nay, answer me. Stand and unfold yourself.
Gerry What?
Eric Barnardo?
Gerry Eric?
Eric You come most carefully upon your hour.
Gerry What?
Eric 'Tis now struck twelve. Get thee to bed.
Gerry Stop pissing about, will you?
Eric (*coming on stage*) Sorry, Gerry. It's in the blood. Can't help it.

Gerry Well, you're too early. The buffet's not ready yet.

Eric Ah. The funeral baked meats did coldly furnish forth the after-play party.

Gerry What?

Eric Never mind.

Gerry Look, I'm trying to sort the food out.

Eric Of course. It's in your blood, too.

Gerry What is?

Eric Stage management. You stage-managed the show and now you're stage-managing the snacks.

Gerry Cuisine, Eric. I've got to get on. Do you mind?

Eric Not at all. Press on.

Gerry Thank you. (*He calls off*) Patsy!

Patsy (*off*) What?

Gerry More.

Patsy What?

Gerry More. Let's have a bit more.

Eric And so say all of us.

Patsy (*off*) A bit more what?

Gerry (*sighing, then shouting*) Open the curtains a bit more!

Patsy (*off*) Oh. Sorry.

The CURTAIN *closes*

Gerry Open them! Open them, woman!

Eric (*with a nod to off stage*) Patsy?

Gerry Who else?

Eric Poor kid.

Gerry Eh?

Eric Patsy. Nigel's not coming, you know.

Gerry No? He's not still seeing Dolly, is he?

Eric He's seeing a lot of Dolly.

Gerry Let's face it: there's a lot of Dolly to see.

They chortle at this

   Patsy's head appears through the CURTAIN

Gerry and Eric stop laughing

Patsy What? Oh, hallo, Eric.
Eric Greetings, nymph.
Gerry I said, open the curtains, Patsy. Open. They're supposed to go outwards.
Patsy Yes, I know, I know.
Gerry Then why did you close them?
Patsy I didn't know I was closing them, Gerry. I thought I was opening them.
Gerry Well, you weren't.
Patsy I've never done it before, you know.
Gerry But it's so bloody easy, Patsy. It's a binary system. (*He moves his hands*) Open—shut. Open—shut.
Eric (*moving his hands*) Or up—down. Up—down. In some cases.
Gerry (*to Eric*) To think I almost asked her to do it for the show.
Eric Really?
Gerry Thank God I didn't. We'd've had the sodding things shut for the performance and open for the scene changes.
Patsy All right. There's no need to snap.
Gerry Right. Sorry. (*Calmly*) Do you think you've cracked it now?
Patsy I think so, yes.
Gerry Good. Then please go and open them a little more.

   Patsy's head disappears

And you can turn the music off. We don't really need it till the others turn up.

   Patsy re-appears

Patsy Pardon?

Gerry I said, would you please turn the music off.

Patsy Don't you like it?

Gerry Yes, I like it. I chose it myself. But we don't need it till the others turn up, though. Do we?

Patsy No, I suppose not.

Patsy disappears. After a while, the music stops

Eric Your choice, was it? The music.

Gerry Yes. Should put people in a relaxed mood. Don't you think?

Eric Really?

Gerry Yes. Why, what's wrong with it?

Eric It doesn't seem to be relaxing you, does it?

Gerry It's not the music that's winding me up, Eric. It's the bloody curtains swishing backwards and forwards.

Eric Quite. By the way, you haven't seen Mrs Tremlett's globe, have you?

Gerry What?

Eric Globe, singular.

Gerry What?

Eric As opposed to globes, plural. It's not a personal question.

Gerry What are you on about?

Eric Apparently she let us borrow her antique globe. She's been round to the dressing rooms asking if she could have it back.

Gerry Oh, honestly. The play's been over for five minutes and she comes nosing round here for her blasted globe.

Eric Yes.

Gerry Tell her to piss off.

Eric Oh, Gerry.

Gerry Daft cow.

Eric Don't be so mean.

Gerry Well.

Eric Anyway, where is it?
Gerry I have no idea. Nor do I care.

The CURTAIN *swishes open to reveal the "Hamlet" set and two tables* L, *spread with party food. There are also some chairs*

Eric (*moving to the tables*) Ah! Food!
Gerry (*slapping Eric's hand*) Keep off.
Eric Oh, come on, Gerry. I'm starving.
Gerry It's not ready yet.

Gerry sets down his clipboard and makes a few adjustments to his food arrangement

Patsy enters with a plastic bag

What's this?
Patsy The bridge rolls.
Eric Bridge rolls! Will we ever get over them?
Patsy Pardon?
Gerry Ignore him, Patsy. (*He looks in the bag*) There's rather a
    lot, isn't there?
Patsy Hmm. I got in a bit of a muddle with them, I'm afraid.
Gerry Oh yes?
Patsy Yes. I gave your message to Martin and then I forgot I'd
    done that and I gave it to Gill, too.
Gerry So we have twice the amount?
Patsy Sorry.
Gerry Never mind, never mind. Let's have a look at them.
Eric I think he means the rolls, Patsy.
Patsy What?
Gerry Shove off, Eric. We've got work to do.

Ophelia enters. She is still wearing her costume

Eric Soft you now. The fair Ophelia.

Ophelia Hallo, Eric. Hallo, you two.

Gerry You'll have to wait if you want a roll.

Ophelia Sorry?

Eric You don't want a roll with Gerry anyway, do you, child?

Ophelia Well...

Eric Come with me and we'll improvise.

He leads her away from the tables. Patsy and Gerry set about arranging the rolls. Patsy sets her rolls out like a line of soldiers. Gerry is much more delicate

   Well. Who would've thought it?

Ophelia Sorry?

Eric You. I mean, you look so young, so innocent, and yet you are clearly very—experienced.

Ophelia Am I?

Eric Aren't you? The skill you brought to Ophelia. The sheer bloody artistry of it.

Ophelia Really? Do you think so?

Eric You were a knock-out.

Ophelia Thank you. Of course, I worked terribly hard at my hands.

Eric Your hands?

Ophelia Yes. I thought they were my most expressive feature.

Eric Oh, they were. Your hands were lovely. Couldn't keep my eyes off them.

Ophelia Really?

Eric Among other things. Such a pity you were getting nothing back.

Ophelia Wasn't I?

Eric From Hamlet. He lacked passion, I thought.

Ophelia Did he?

Eric Shame, really, because it's there in you. I sense it. You wanted a Hamlet that was burning up with desire for you.

Ophelia I see.

Eric But he was lacking in physicality. If I'd been playing the role…

Ophelia You?

Eric Yes. I would've gone for the pent-up desire.

Ophelia Pent-up?

Eric Partly pent-up. Occasionally bursting out. He shouldn't be able to keep his hands off you. Don't you think?

Alice enters (possibly with one or two others). She fixes a beady eye on Eric

Ophelia Well…

Eric Of course, an actress with artistic soul would respond to that. After all, you don't just act with your mouth, do you?

Ophelia Don't you?

Eric (*edging closer to her*) Your body's got to come into it somewhere, hasn't it?

Alice makes her move

Alice Hallo, there.

Eric (*not disguising his disappointment*) Oh. Hallo, Alice.

Alice May I join you?

Ophelia Do. Please.

Alice Well. This is cosy. Are we the first?

Ophelia I think so. Some of the others said they were going down the pub, actually.

Alice Really? Don't tell Gerry. He'll have a fit. (*She pauses*) So…

Eric Yes.

Alice I think we got away with it, don't you?

Ophelia Hmm?

Alice *Hamlet.* I think it sort of—came off.

Ophelia Came off? You think it did?

Eric Not really. It's just the way he wears his tights.

Alice (*warning him*) Eric.

Ophelia How do you mean?

Eric (*smiling*) Well, Alice said it sort of came off, and I said——

Alice Don't be smutty, Eric.

Eric Smutty? *Moi?*

Alice (*to Ophelia*) Smutty men are so sad, don't you think?

Ophelia Well, I——

Alice His brain locked at fourteen, you know, but we're an open-minded group. We try not to hold it against him.

Eric (*smirking at Ophelia*) Take no notice, child. You can hold it against me anytime——

Alice No, Eric!

Alice leads Ophelia upstage. Eric sighs and follows. During the following exchanges, they greet various non-speaking actors who may be there, talk quietly, drink, perhaps wander on and off

Patsy (*gesturing at the tables*) How's this?

Gerry Well. Do you think you could be a bit more...

Patsy What?

Gerry Artistic.

Patsy How do you mean?

Gerry Use a bit of flair, a bit of arrangement.

Patsy Evening classes, you mean.

Gerry No, I mean——

Patsy I'd like to, Gerry, but I already go to evening classes——

Gerry No, no. I mean now. The bridge rolls.

Patsy Eh?

Gerry The way you've dumped the rolls down. Couldn't you

make patterns with them? Make them look more attractive?
Like mine.

Patsy Oh. I see. I'll have a go.

Patsy begins to build a tower of rolls. Gerry watches for a while

Is this better?

Gerry Well... The trouble is you've got too many. Tell you what.
Eat a couple.

Patsy I'm not hungry.

Gerry Oh, come on. Eat a couple, and then you can make
something artistic out of the rest.

Patsy What's in them?

Gerry What difference does that make?

Patsy If it's egg, I throw up. I can't help it.

Gerry Well, it shouldn't be egg. What did you tell Martin?

Patsy Ham, I think.

Gerry It's ham, then.

Patsy (*disappointedly*) Oh. What about these?

Gerry They're mine.

Patsy And they're...?

Gerry Ham.

Patsy They're not all ham, are they?

Gerry They are, as a matter of fact.

Patsy Why?

Gerry Isn't it obvious?

Patsy Is it?

Gerry Because of the play.

Patsy Oh, I see. (*She does not really see*) Because of the play.

Gerry Ham. Get it?

Patsy Ham, yes. Mind you, we're a bit stuck if people don't like
ham, aren't we?

Gerry Why shouldn't they like it?

Patsy Well, Nigel had a dodgy sausage once.

Gerry Yes, I've heard about Nigel's dodgy sausage.

Patsy What?

Gerry Never mind.

Patsy Anyway, it turned quite funny on him.

Gerry Really?

Patsy He was hanging over our toilet for the best part of two days.

Gerry You plan to go round telling people that, do you?

Patsy I'm only saying——

Gerry Anyway, it's ham we're on about, not sausages.

Patsy It amounts to the same, though, doesn't it?

Gerry I mean, I chose ham because if its special relevance.

Patsy Yes. Of course. (*She realizes what he means*) Oh, I see. Ham.

Gerry Yes.

Patsy Because of the acting, you mean.

Gerry What?

Patsy Ham. Acting. A kind of joke.

Gerry No, it's not because——

Patsy You don't think people will take offence?

Gerry Not because of the acting, Patsy. Because of the play.

Patsy The play?

Gerry Hamlet.

Patsy Yes?

Gerry Ham. Let.

Patsy Oh yes. Very good, Gerry. That's very clever. (*She does not understand*) Do you think they'll get it?

Gerry Of course they will. Now just eat a couple and then we can get on. Right?

Patsy Right. (*She takes a roll from Gerry's display and eats it*)

Gerry Not mine, you pilchard.

Patsy (*eating*) Why not?

Gerry I had a perfect sunburst there. You've cocked up the symmetry.

Patsy Sorry.

Gerry Eat your own bloody rolls.

Patsy Sorry, sorry.

Gerry Well. You've got yours lined up like men in a urinal, and you have to take one of mine. Use your head, will you?

Patsy Does it really matter?

Gerry Of course it does. People like to be attracted by what they eat. You have to seduce them.

Patsy With ham rolls?

Gerry With the look of them. With the arrangement.

Alice wanders over from the other group

Alice Ah. Grub.

Gerry Grub?

Alice Smashing. (*She attempts to take a roll*)

Gerry (*slapping her hand*) Not yet, not yet. God, you're a pig sometimes, Alice.

Alice Sorry.

Gerry What does this say to you?

Alice Pardon?

Gerry Come. Take me. Let me lure you into a nibble. Let me flirt with your taste buds.

Alice Not on an empty stomach, Gerry.

Gerry The food, the food. Look at hers. Like a bloody jumble sale.

Alice Well…

Gerry Now. Can you see what I'm trying to say with my ham roll sunburst here? Aren't you tempted?

Alice I am a bit peckish, yes.

Gerry Well, you'll have to wait.

Alice Oh.

Gerry We've got to get this right. Eat a couple more, Patsy.

Alice I will, if you like.

Gerry Were you asked to muster the cuisine?

Alice I thought you said——

Gerry Patsy and I are in charge here. I'll tell you when you can get your nose in the trough. All right?

Alice All right. Keep your hair on.

Gerry Push off, then.

Alice I'm going. Oh, by the way. I've just seen Mrs Tremlett, and——

Gerry I know, I know. She can whistle for her bloody globe. Now, push off.

Alice (*going back to the others*) Sorry. Sorry I spoke.

Gerry And start the tape, will you? So people can loosen up a little.

Alice (*not stopping*) Loosen up? Fall apart more like.

Gerry Come on, Patsy. We can't spoil the ship for a ha'p'orth of tar. (*He hands her some rolls*) Here, get yourself outside those.

Patsy hesitates

Come on, come on.

Patsy stuffs a roll into her mouth. Gerry checks his list

Hell-fire! Look at the peanuts!

Patsy (*with a full mouth*) What's wrong with them?

Gerry They're still in the bloody bags. Why must I do everything myself?

Patsy Well, where should they be?

Gerry What?

Patsy Where should they be?

Gerry In bowls, of course. Where are the bowls? Get these bloody peanuts in some bowls, will you?

Patsy charges round and finds a large plastic bowl. She offers it to Gerry

(*Not moving*) What's this?
Patsy (*trying to swallow*) A bowl.
Gerry This is no good.
Patsy No?
Gerry Of course not. Look at it, Patsy. I mean, just look at it.

Patsy takes it and examines it

It might do for a pee, but it's not the slightest sodding use for a peanut. Get rid of it. Find something a touch more delicate.

Patsy looks for somewhere to put the bowl. She cannot find a suitable place, so she runs to the exit

Kate enters. Patsy almost knocks her over

Kate Oh, Patsy. You haven't seen——
Patsy Sorry, can't stop.

Patsy exits

Kate watches Gerry as he tries to open a bag of nuts. They do not open. He has his back to us and is doubled up with the effort

Kate Gerry!
Gerry Not now, not now, Kate. Can't you see I'm busy?
Kate (*to Alice*) What is he up to?
Alice Problems with his nuts, I think.
Kate (*moving over to Alice and the others*) You haven't seen that globe, have you?

"In The Hall Of The Mountain King" starts to play, gradually gaining in ferocity

Patsy enters, running. She finds a delicate bowl on Gerry's table. It already has nuts in it. She tries to eat a handful

Gerry Open, you bastards! Open! (*He throws the packet down, breathing heavily*)

Patsy cannot eat all the peanuts from Gerry's bowl. In a moment of panic, she tosses the nuts behind the table. Gerry resumes his attack on the bag of peanuts. Patsy stands, still chewing, with her empty bowl ready. Suddenly, the bag splits and peanuts shower everywhere

You buggers! You heartless little buggers!
Patsy (*thrusting the bowl at him*) Here.
Gerry Quick, quick. Pick them up.

They get on their hands and knees, and scoop up peanuts, dropping them in the bowl

Patsy Oh, dear. They're a bit dirty, Gerry.
Gerry Never mind, never mind.
Patsy I'm getting bits with mine. Shall I——
Gerry No! Just scoop them up. (*Finishing*) Right. Perfect. (*He notices the bowl*) Ah, this is good. It'll match mine. Where did you get it from?
Patsy Well, it was... (*For fear of giving the game away, she snatches up another roll and crams it in her mouth*)
Gerry Yes, yes. You're right. We'd better sort these out.

"In The Hall Of The Mountain King" is now quite frenetic. Gerry tries to make a speedy arrangement of rolls on Patsy's table. Patsy chews wearily. Gerry hands her more rolls to eat. She stuffs another in her mouth, but she cannot eat as quickly as he supplies them

Faster, faster.

Patsy (*with a full mouth*) I can't.

Gerry Oh, Patsy. You're hopeless. (*He puts a roll in each pocket, then picks up two more. There are still too many. He throws off the last two*)

Patsy and Gerry are both quite breathless. Kate and Alice join them

Alice I've already asked him, but he wasn't very receptive.

Kate Gerry, you haven't seen——

Gerry Kate! Super to see you.

Alice You haven't seen the globe, have you, Gerry?

Gerry God, not again.

Alice Told you.

Gerry Why is everyone so obsessed with Old Ma Tremlett's bloody globe?

Kate Probably because it's worth——

Gerry Look, there are far more important things in life than that old bat's knick-knacks.

Patsy Actually, Kate, I think it's——

Gerry Patsy!

Patsy Yes?

Gerry Another roll.

Patsy Right. (*She takes another roll and chews it in subdued silence*)

Kate (*to Alice*) He knows something.

Gerry What the bloody hell has happened to the music? (*To Patsy*) Didn't you rewind the tape?

Patsy (*with her mouth full*) You didn't say——

Gerry What?

Patsy I said——

Gerry Never mind, I'll sort it out myself.

Gerry exits

Kate smiles at Patsy who smiles back. Her cheeks are stuffed with ham roll

Kate You were about to say?
Patsy (*almost inaudibly*) Sorry?
Kate Sorry?
Alice The globe, Patsy. Where is it?
Patsy (*still chewing*) The globe. There was a bit of a hitch——
Kate (*interrupting, not having understood*) Never mind.
Alice (*nodding at the table*) We've started, then, have we?
Patsy Started?
Alice The food.
Patsy Hmm.
Kate Yes. I suppose you really work up an appetite taking goblets on and off all evening.
Alice You do if Gerry's in charge. (*She goes to the table and looks at the food*)

"In The Hall Of The Mountain King" stops, and "Morning" starts again

During the following, Eric and Ophelia discreetly detach themselves from the others and engage in deep conversation

Bridge rolls.
Patsy Hmm.
Alice Can't stand bridge rolls. Never know whether to eat them or wipe the make-up off with them.
Patsy Hmm?
Alice I mean, they're cotton wool, aren't they?

Gerry enters

They all stand silent for a moment

Gerry Well...
Kate Hallo, Gerry.
Gerry This is—nice.
Patsy Hmm.
Alice Yes.
Gerry Well...
Kate What?
Gerry Don't just stand there. (*He indicates the food*) Have
   something to nibble. Have a roll.
Alice What's in them?
Gerry (*with a short laugh*) Funny you should ask that...
Alice Is it? Why?
Gerry They're ham.
Kate Oh, really?
Gerry Yes. Ham, get it?
Kate Sorry?
Gerry Ham. (*Desperately*) Ham. Let.
Kate Oh.
Patsy It's a joke. Sort of.
Kate Yes. (*She does not understand*) I'll have a few nuts, I think.
Alice You haven't got any gooseberries, have you?
Gerry What?
Alice (*nodding in the direction of Eric and Ophelia*) I think I
   ought to take something over to those two. (*She takes a plate
   and moves over to them*) Fancy some of Gerry's nibbles?
Eric No.
Ophelia Lovely.

Alice leads Ophelia forward. Eric sighs and follows them

Pause

Alice Well.

Eric Yes?

Alice *Hamlet*. Quite an achievement when you think about it.

Ophelia Oh. Yes. Nice costumes.

Eric You thought so?

Ophelia Well, weren't they?

Eric They're all right if you know how to wear them.

Ophelia Really?

Eric It's a matter of body acting, isn't it? I mean, Horatio looked as if he was wearing Pampers.

Alice Hmm. I suppose there's an art to acting in tights.

Patsy, still chewing, joins them. From time to time, she picks things off Alice's plate

Eric There is, there is. And he hasn't got it. And what about Laertes?

Patsy Who?

Eric That ponce with the fashionable trousers.

Alice You mean Kevin.

Eric I've never heard such an obvious dry. Gertrude goes on and on for five minutes about Ophelia drowning. How she chucks herself in the river and goes bobbing downstream. And what does Laertes say? "Alas, then she is drowned." I thought to myself: "No, sunshine; she was shot." I ask you. Was that the best he could come up with?

Ophelia I think you'll find that is the actual line, Eric.

Eric What? "Alas, then she is drowned"?

Ophelia I believe so.

Eric Rubbish.

Alice Well, in my version——

Eric Look, we're talking about Shakespeare here, my dear. He was the John Godber of his day, he was, and he wouldn't come up with a line as stupid as that. Whereas Kevin Flash-Pants would.

Patsy I see what you mean. It's a bit strange really, isn't it?
Alice What is?
Patsy Falling in the river without getting wet.

The other three stare at her, puzzled

Ophelia What?
Patsy I mean, in she goes, and she must've gone right under, and yet she was completely dry.
Ophelia Was I?
Patsy It doesn't make sense, does it? You don't expect Shakespeare to make a mistake like that.
Alice What are you on about?
Patsy What's-'er-name? Delia.
Eric Delia?
Patsy Drowned but completely dry.
Eric Not her, you clot. Laertes.
Patsy Laertes?
Alice Kevin.
Patsy Well, he didn't fall in, did he? Unless I missed something.
Eric Of course he didn't fall in. He dried.
Ophelia I don't think he did.
Patsy But how could he dry if he wasn't wet?
Eric He dried. Dried. Forgot his lines.
Patsy Oh.
Ophelia Except that he didn't.
Eric You missed something all right, Patsy.
Patsy Yes. I expect so.

Pause

Funny music.
Alice Hilarious.
Patsy Gerry says it's supposed to relax us.

Alice Well it's getting right up my nose. I think I'll turn it off.

Alice exits

Eric I can't stand bossy women, can you?
Ophelia Alice, you mean?
Eric It goes against nature.
Patsy Ah. I don't agree with you there, Eric.
Eric No?
Patsy No. I've been doing these evening classes——
Ophelia Really? What on?
Patsy What's-name. Aggression.
Eric Aggression?
Patsy Something like that.
Ophelia Assertiveness?
Patsy That's it. Have you heard of it?
Eric Assertiveness, my arse.
Patsy No, really——
Eric Castration, more like. I suppose they're all women.
Patsy They are as a matter of fact. I wouldn't want to do it with
  men around.
Ophelia Well, I think it's a good thing.
Eric Cobblers.
Ophelia No, really. You have to give vent to your feelings. You
  shouldn't keep it all bottled up.
Patsy That's what Nigel says.
Eric He would.

The music stops

Alice enters

Patsy He fixed it up for me. Tuesday nights. I leave him his tea
  and then he goes out with the lads and I go off to this course.

Alice (*looking at the empty plate*) Oh. None left.
Patsy Oh, yes. Sorry.
Alice Fetch us some more, will you?
Patsy Yes. Of course.

Patsy trots over to Gerry and Kate. They ignore her. Eric, Alice and Ophelia rejoin the non-speaking party-goers

Kate Still. On the whole it went quite well.
Gerry Oh, yes.
Kate There were hiccups, of course.
Gerry There are always hiccups, Kate.
Patsy Like Kevin.
Kate What?
Patsy Being dry when he should have been wet.
Kate Yes. (*She gives Gerry a puzzled look*) I am pleased, though. Overall.
Gerry I'm pleased you're pleased, Kate. Excellent. We did ourselves proud, don't you think?
Kate Oh yes. It must've, you know, enhanced our reputation.
Patsy Oh yes.
Gerry Certainly. Certainly it has. I mean, that was a professional display. I don't think it's unfair to say that, do you?
Patsy Oh, no.
Kate It's what I always aim for.
Gerry Slick, efficient. We were completely on top of the whole thing.
Kate As was Eric. By all accounts.
Gerry Oh yes.

They laugh, though Patsy is not sure why

  Mind you...
Kate Yes?

Gerry The play wasn't so hot.

Kate The play?

Gerry Just between you and me. I mean it could've been a shade less...

Kate What?

Gerry Well, patchy. Slack. In places.

Kate Patchy?

Gerry Shame, really. Superb set, wonderful scene changes.

Patsy Yes.

Gerry Really, really good. And bloody awful acting.

Kate Oh, come off it, Gerry. They were quite good. Some of them.

Gerry Quite good? Dear, oh, dear. They were pathetic.

Kate What about Eric on Friday night.

Patsy Oh yes.

Gerry Eric?

Kate As the ghost. He was absolutely spectral.

Gerry He was as spectral as a newt, Kate, and I think you know it.

Kate Look, Gerry, I think I know...

Gerry What's up?

Kate There's something wrong with these nuts.

Gerry Now what?

Kate Taste as if there's grit in them.

Patsy There probably is. We——

Gerry It's sea salt. OK?

Kate Sea salt?

Gerry Yes.

Patsy Yes. (*Pause*) Alice says you were looking for the globe.

Kate Yes?

Patsy I shouldn't worry too much about it, Kate.

Kate Why?

Gerry Very healthy, sea salt.

Patsy I happened to have this what's-name.

Kate This what?

Patsy Super-glue.

Kate You what?

Patsy You'd hardly know. Really, you wouldn't. I mean, if you just glanced at it you'd think they were rivers.

Gerry Patsy.

Kate What were rivers?

Patsy The cracks.

Gerry Look, Patsy——

Kate What's happened?

Gerry Nothing.

Patsy It was quite funny, really. At the time.

Kate What happened?

Patsy Gerry kicked it.

Kate He what?

Patsy Kicked it. You should've seen it——

Gerry I didn't kick it, Patsy. I tripped over it.

Patsy That's right. Tripped.

Gerry Brushed against it with my foot. It wasn't on the chart, you see.

Kate The globe wasn't on the chart? What are you saying, Gerry?

Gerry My chart. Every prop and every piece of furniture has to go down on my chart. Old Ma Tremlett's globe turned up out of the blue. It had no place. It was surplus requirements——

Kate It wasn't. It was perfectly in keeping.

Gerry It was a mistake, Kate. Like chucking a spare cog into a well-oiled machine.

Kate Gerry, it was worth five hundred pounds.

Gerry (*after a brief stunned silence; quietly*) What?

Patsy Oh, dear.

Kate It was an antique.

Gerry Then why did the stupid cow lend it to us?

Kate Because I persuaded her.

Gerry That was a wee bit silly, if you don't mind me saying so.

Kate How was I to know you'd take a flying kick at it?

Gerry I didn't take a flying kick——

Patsy Well——

Gerry Shut up, Patsy. Someone put it where it shouldn't've been and I tripped over it.

Kate Tripped?

Patsy And it went soaring into the stalls.

Kate It what?

Gerry It trickled off the stage.

Patsy Well, I wouldn't say——

Gerry Patsy! Will you shut up!

Patsy flinches

Have a roll.

Gerry takes a roll from his pocket and gives it to her. Patsy is cowed and starts meekly to chew it

Where the hell is the rest of the cast? We should be in full swing by now.

Kate If that globe is damaged, Gerry——

Gerry Of course it's not damaged.

Kate —we're done for. Ruined.

Gerry Look, the old bat can have her globe back. She won't notice a thing. It's perfectly all right. Isn't it, Patsy?

Patsy (*with her mouth full*) Hmm.

Gerry I mean the glues they come up with these days. Absolutely marvellous. It's stronger than it's ever been before. Tell her, Patsy.

Patsy (*swallowing*) Oh yes.

Gerry See?

Patsy Mind you...

Kate What?

Patsy Well, I sort of propped it on my beaker to dry...

Kate Yes?

Patsy You know those beakers you get with those flasks?

Kate Yes.

Patsy Thermos flasks. The ones they do in Boots——

Gerry We know what a bloody flask is, Patsy. What have you done?

Patsy Nothing.

Kate Nothing?

Patsy Well, I tried standing it on the table, but it kept rolling off. The globe, I mean, not the flask. So I got the beaker and stood it on that.

Kate Yes?

Patsy You know, like a golf tee. And that seemed to do the trick. I thought that was quite clever of me.

Gerry Brilliant.

Patsy You know what's-name? Horizontal thinking.

Gerry (*trying to stay calm*) So you have super-glued a plastic beaker to Old Ma Tremlett's globe, have you, Patsy?

Patsy You can get replacements. Without buying the whole thing.

Gerry Replacement beakers?

Patsy Yes.

Gerry Yes. I thought that's what you meant.

Patsy (*laughing weakly*) You'd smile to see it, Kate. You really would.

Gerry God help us.

Patsy (*nervously*) It looks as if it's got a nose.

Kate I don't believe this.

Gerry (*to Kate*) You see what I have to put up with? (*To Patsy*) Didn't you realize, you pilchard; that globe was antique?

Patsy Well...

Gerry Poor old Mrs Tremlett loved that globe.

Patsy Well, you kicked it in the first place.

Gerry I did not kick it!

Patsy (*tearfully*) You did. You said a rude word and booted it into the stalls.

Kate That's it. Ruined. Done for. Finished.

Gerry Oh, don't be such a misery. If you hadn't brought the sodding thing along——

Kate Don't blame me.

Gerry Well, it's not my fault, is it? I didn't stick a bloody beaker to it, did I?

Patsy It doesn't look too bad, Kate. Honestly.

Kate Oh, really, Patsy. How can it not look too bad?

Patsy It's round the back.

Gerry Round the back? Round the back? What are you on about?

Patsy On Australia. People might not notice it there. If she keeps it to the wall.

Gerry Give me strength.

Kate What am I going to tell her? What am I going to tell the woman?

Gerry Look, let's keep calm about this, shall we?

Kate Calm, calm? Five hundred pounds worth of globe? It'll ruin us.

Gerry Possibly not. Let's take a cool and considered look at it and assess the damage. Patsy?

Patsy Yes, Gerry?

Gerry Fetch the globe. We'll see what we can do.

Patsy Yes, Gerry.

Patsy exits to fetch the globe. She bundles past Alice as she goes

Alice Where's she off to?

Kate To fetch the globe.

Alice Ah, it's turned up, then?

Kate Oh, it's turned up all right. Paul Gascoigne here booted it into the auditorium.

Alice He what?

Kate Smashed it to bits.

Gerry Oh, come on, Kate. You're getting hysterical.

Kate We're ruined, Alice. Ruined. We can't possibly afford to pay for it.

Alice Oh, Gerry.

Gerry Why must you always look on the black side? All right, there's been a hitch——

Kate Bloody vandal.

Gerry —but there's not a problem that doesn't have a solution.

Patsy enters with the globe

Patsy Here it is.

Alice Good grief. What's that?

Patsy It's my beaker.

Alice It looks like a nose.

Patsy That's what I said. You have to laugh, really, don't you?

Gerry Right. Let's have a look.

They place it on one of the tables and gather around it like doctors

Yes... I'm sure we can do something here. Patsy!

Patsy Yes?

Gerry Stanley knife.

Patsy Who?

Gerry Stanley knife, Patsy. Fetch me my knife.

Patsy Oh. Right!

Patsy exits

Eric and Ophelia move down stage

Eric It's body acting, as I said.

Ophelia Body acting?

Eric Yes. I'll show you what I mean. The bit where it says she should become a nun, right?

Ophelia Get thee to a nunnery?

Eric That's the bit. What's the thinking behind that, do you reckon?

Ophelia The thinking?

Eric Yes. Why is he telling her to become a nun?

Ophelia Well... Because he doesn't want her corrupted.

Eric Nice try, but I don't think so.

Ophelia No?

Eric No. Not when she's already corrupt.

Ophelia Is she?

Eric But of course. They're lovers, remember. They've enjoyed each other.

Ophelia I'm not sure...

Eric Of course they have. No, he doesn't really want her to shut herself away in a convent.

Ophelia No?

Eric No. He wants her to dress up as a nun. See?

Ophelia I see. Why should he want her to do that?

Eric This is what I'm driving at. It turns him on, see. The contrast of flesh and innocence. Body acting.

Ophelia I was trying for something like that. With my hands.

Eric Hands are not enough, though, are they? He's barely in control of his passion at this stage. He has more than hands on his mind. I'll show you what I mean. A little impro. I'm Hamlet, right?

Ophelia Right.

Eric And you're Ophelia. OK?

Eric strikes a pose as the moody Dane. Ophelia looks a little uncertain

Get thee to a nunnery!

Ophelia Right.

Eric Put thee on thyself the habit of a nun.

Ophelia But he doesn't actually say that...

Eric What? No, no, not in so many words. But this is impro, isn't it?

Ophelia I see.

Eric You have to go with it. Respond as the mood takes you.

Ophelia Right.

Eric Go on, then.

Ophelia Oh, yes. Of course. (*She swings her arms a bit, not sure what to do*)

Eric (*approaching her*) I would have thee in the habit of a nun.

Ophelia (*looking around nervously*) I—er—I haveth not any habit about me, my lord.

Patsy enters, carrying the Stanley knife. She rejoins the group around the table

Eric (*clasping her*) It matters not, sweet Ophelia. It's in your mind. Thy mind. Thou hast the body of a woman but I wouldest thou came on as a nun.

Ophelia A nun?

Eric Yes. Yea.

Ophelia Right. (*After a little thought, she puts her hands together in prayer*) Like this you mean?

Eric Well, a bit like that. Only more sensual. Like the one on the bottle.

Ophelia Sorry?

Eric You know, that blue nun. All demure, but begging for it with her eyes.

Ophelia Oh, the wine bottle.

Eric That's it. Now, what you're giving me here is the demureness. And what the text requires is a kind of throbbing within.

Ophelia A throbbing?

Eric Yes. Can you give me that?

Ophelia I'll try. (*Still clasping her hands together, she rocks backwards and forwards*)

Eric Yes, yes. You're getting there. It's a start, anyway. (*He continues as Hamlet*) Oh, Ophelia, let me take you away from all this.

Ophelia Pardon?

Eric All this misery. My bent uncle and your prying father.

Ophelia Polonius.

Eric What?

Ophelia Polonius. My father.

Eric Oh, yes. Of course. We two can maketh a world of our own.

Ophelia I think I'm getting there, Eric.

Eric Hamlet.

Ophelia I mean Hamlet. But I feel...

Eric What?

Ophelia I feel the music would help. Don't you?

Eric No, no. Don't bother.

Ophelia It's all right. I don't mind.

Eric We don't really need the music, child.

Ophelia (*hurrying to exit*) Won't take a sec.

Ophelia exits

After a moment, "In The Hall Of The Mountain King" starts again

The non-speaking party-goers could exit to go to the pub at this point

Gerry It's coming. I do believe it's coming.

Kate Careful, careful.

Alice Just a little more.

Gerry Patsy.

Patsy Yes?

Gerry Mop my brow. Quick.

Ophelia enters and joins Eric again in their improvisation

Patsy Yes, Gerry. (*She looks around, snatches up a roll, and mops his brow*)
Gerry (*triumphantly*) Got it.

The music ends. They turn around, and Gerry holds up the globe in one hand and the beaker in the other

Patsy Oh, well done, Gerry!

Patsy hugs him, and he drops the globe. Alice catches it

Gerry Get off me, woman!
Kate Oh, well held.
Gerry Get her off me!
Patsy Sorry, Gerry. I was just so pleased.
Gerry You soft tart——
Alice All right. It's all right.
Patsy You have to express your feelings. That's what they tell us——

During the following, Eric grabs Ophelia and pulls her to him

Gerry Not all over me, you don't.
Kate Look, never mind. Let's have a look at it.

The four of them gather around to examine the globe. From here the two scenes run together like one

Eric Go with it. Yield to the feeling.
Alice I don't think you could tell, you know.

Ophelia I am a nun. Burning with passion...
Eric Yes, yes.
Kate I think we might get away with this.
Eric Yield.
Patsy It's going to be a bit rough on the lips, though.
Gerry What?
Eric Consummation...
Patsy Where the glue's dried. It's gone all hard.
Eric I can certainly feel something.
Alice What are you on about?
Ophelia Yes. And I feel she would respond——
Eric Yes?
Ophelia —quite physically.
Patsy I don't think I should take the risk.
Gerry What?
Eric Throw caution to the wind, child.
Patsy It might stick to my lips.
Alice (*setting the globe on a chair*) We're talking about the globe, Patsy.
Patsy Oh.
Gerry We don't give a toss about the bloody beaker.
Eric Respond, then. Give, give.
Ophelia Yes!

Ophelia takes a mighty swing and belts Eric round the face. The group around the globe all turn to look

Eric Ow!
Ophelia Yes. I see what you mean. It feels so—right.
Eric What the hell did you do that for?
Ophelia It's the way I felt I should respond. Physically.
Eric It bloody well hurt.
Ophelia The power. The passion.

Ophelia swings her arms, Eric flinches back and is about to sit on the globe. Kate whips it away just in time, passing it to Alice like a ball out of a scrum

Kate Watch out!
Eric What?
Alice (*passing the globe to Gerry*) Watch where you're sitting.
Eric She just bloody hit me.
Gerry (*passing the globe to Patsy*) Patsy.
Ophelia (*distractedly*) This is wonderful. You don't think with your head. You think with your body.
Gerry What's she on about?
Eric Don't ask me. Silly bitch.
Patsy Don't work it out. React.
Kate What?
Patsy She's right. That's what they tell me in my evening classes.
Ophelia Don't accept things.

Patsy moves to Ophelia

Patsy Don't be inhibited.
Ophelia Don't be a nun if you don't want to be!
Gerry A nun?
Patsy That's what Nigel says. But I don't have to be!
Ophelia Don't be put down.
Patsy Or pushed around.
Gerry Patsy, sit down and——
Patsy (*boldly defying him*) No!
Ophelia From the centre of your being you feel, you know how to respond.
Patsy Yes!
Ophelia Respond physically.
Patsy Yes, yes.
Ophelia Do something!
Patsy Yes!
Kate No, Patsy. Don't!

Patsy dashes the globe to the floor and it shatters. Silently, they all look from the debris to Patsy

Gerry (*quietly*) You—pilchard.

Patsy Oh dear.

Kate (*stooping to pick up the pieces*) We're finished. Ruined.

Patsy Sorry, Kate.

Ophelia No, no. It was my fault.

Kate This was our last performance. We've had it.

Gerry You mean—financially.

Kate Financially. Artistically. In every possible way. It's the end of the line. Drama ends here.

Eric The rest is silence.

Gerry (*slumping in a chair*) Well…

Kate Well what?

Gerry Well, I mean, too bad.

Eric Too bad?

Gerry Yes. Tough. But in the end, I mean, so what?

Ophelia So what?

Gerry Yes. I'm sick of it all anyway. It's just aggravation and toil and heartache——

Ophelia But it's theatre, Gerry.

Gerry You bust a gut to build a set and fix the lights and half the time the actors cock it up anyway.

Eric I say——

Gerry So maybe it's not such a bad thing. Maybe this is just what we all need. An excuse to pack it all in.

Ophelia You can't. You can't say that.

Kate Why not? He's probably right. It's all a waste of time. (*She holds up the pieces*) This is all it comes to in the end.

Eric People need theatre, Kate.

Kate Then why don't they come? Because they don't.

Ophelia Some did.

Kate Yes, some did. But I was related to half of them.

Pause. They are all depressed

Alice We'll have to pay. For the globe, I mean. We can't just——
Kate We can't afford it, Alice. It'll take every penny we've got and it still won't be enough.
Ophelia Perhaps we can raise some money.
Kate How? How are we going to raise that much?
Alice A jumble sale?
Gerry }
Kate } (*together*) No.

Pause

Patsy (*brightly*) Well, we could——
Kate What?
Patsy Nothing.
Gerry We could what, Patsy?
Patsy I was just thinking. We could put a play on.

They all look at her in silence

   Well, perhaps not.
Eric Unless… Unless it was something that people really wanted to see.
Ophelia And cheap. A very basic production.
Alice With no overheads. By someone dead.
Ophelia No copyright.
Patsy And something a bit more jolly, without people getting stabbed and poisoned all over the place.
Ophelia Chekhov!
Patsy It was only a thought.
Ophelia No, I mean Chekhov. *The Cherry Orchard.*
Gerry I'm not building a bloody orchard.
Kate *The Cherry Orchard* is not jolly.

Patsy I was thinking more of something like *All Creatures Great And Small*.

Gerry With bloody cows? And bloody sheep?

Patsy You could use puppets.

Kate No.

Eric No. You want something with a bit of glamour. A row of chorus girls——

Alice In black stockings and suspenders?

Eric Why not?

Alice Because we're not here to fuel your puerile fantasies, Eric.

Gerry Besides, you only have to look down the membership list.

Alice I beg your pardon?

Eric (*glancing at Ophelia*) Well, there's——

Ophelia (*sharply*) Yes?

Eric I mean, there's Dolly.

Alice You mean *Moby Dick*?

Gerry All singing, all dancing.

Kate No, no. It's just not on.

Gerry No?

Kate No. If you're going to put on a play, you have to do something you really want to do.

Gerry Like?

Kate Like—*Starlight Express*.

"In The Hall Of The Mountain King" begins to play quietly as they gain in enthusiasm

Ophelia *Starlight Express*?

Kate But with simple staging. Content, not show.

Gerry You can't stage *Starlight Express* simply, Kate. You can't do it.

Eric You'd have to have metallic costumes. Lurex or something, and conical bras.

Ophelia (*making full use of her hands*) And proper arm move-
     ments. You know, part skating, part train——

Alice And Dolly on roller-skates! Yes!

Gerry We'd need a pretty solid track.

Alice We'd need a fly-over.

Kate A completely relevant production. Power and idealism.

*Gerry jumps on a chair to test its strength. Then he begins to
improvise with tables etc.*

Gerry Patsy, clear that table, will you? (*To Eric*) You could build
     a platform from stage left to the top of the Gents, I suppose.

Eric Out over the auditorium?

Gerry Yes, of course.

Alice And Dolly thundering over their heads! Yes!

Kate With some kind of safety net, perhaps.

Alice Borrowed from a trawler.

Ophelia And the lighting would have to be really good.
     Greens——

Gerry And reds. We'd need a set of bloody signals!

Kate Red for danger! Red for power and rage and passion!

Eric Passion! Yes!

Gerry Patsy!

Patsy Yes, Gerry?

Gerry Fetch me my notebook.

Patsy Yes, Gerry.

*There is a bustle of activity and enthusiasm on stage. Before
Patsy can leave, they all freeze. The music swells*

CURTAIN

FURNITURE AND PROPERTY LIST

The play takes place on the setting for *Hamlet*, designed at the director's discretion

On stage: 2 tables. *On them:* arrangements of party food and drink, inc. peanuts in a bag and in a bowl
Chairs
Plastic bowl

Off stage: Clipboard (**Gerry**)
Plastic bag. *In it:* ham rolls (**Patsy**)
Globe with a beaker stuck on it (**Patsy**)
Stanley knife (**Patsy**)

LIGHTING PLOT

Property and practical fittings required: nil
Interior. The same throughout

To open: Overall general lighting

No cues

EFFECTS PLOT

Cue 1   To open   (Page 1)
            "Morning" from Peer Gynt—or similar

Cue 2   After **Patsy** disappears   (Page 4)
            Cut music

Cue 3   **Kate**: "You haven't seen that globe, have you?" (Page 13)
            Music: "In The Hall Of The Mountain King"

Cue 4   **Alice**: "You do if Gerry's in charge."   (Page 16)
            Change music to "Morning"

Cue 5   **Eric**: "He would."   (Page 20)
            Cut music

Cue 6   After **Ophelia** exits   (Page 30)
            Music: "In The Hall Of The Mountain King"

Cue 7   **Gerry**: "Got it."   (Page 31)
            Music ends

Cue 8   **Kate**: "Like—*Starlight Express*."   (Page 36)
            Fade up "In The Hall Of The Mountain King"

Cue 9   They all freeze   (Page 37)
            Music swells